ADVENTURES

of an

OLD LADY
PIANO TEACHER

VICKI KING

ISBN 978-1-63814-447-2 (Paperback)
ISBN 978-1-63814-448-9 (Digital)

Covenant Books, Inc.
11661 Hwy 707
Murrells Inlet, SC 29576
www.covenantbooks.com

This book is dedicated to my husband, Thomas King, who has given me so much to laugh about for so many years!

Introduction

Over the years, I've taught hundreds of piano students, and each one was different. Each one prompted a unique story, and this book is a compilation of those stories and some of the adventures I've encountered in my years as a professional pianist, piano teacher, and organist.

Why an old lady piano teacher? When I was a child, all the piano teachers I knew seemed old to me as they had gray hair and glasses. Several years ago, I was judging in Texas for the National Guild of Piano Teachers. A six-year-old boy walked in the room dressed up for his piano audition, wearing a fancy bow tie. He had prepared several pieces. After the first one, I explained that I would be writing on his evaluation card for a few minutes before going on to the next piece. While I was writing, he was staring intently at me and said, "You know, you're really old!" (As if I had not noticed!)

"Yes," I said, "it's important to have old judges. Old judges are very wise."

"Yes, but you're old enough—you could be a grandmother!" he exclaimed. Needless to say, I had to give careful thought as to what I would say on his evaluation! So now that I really am an "old lady" with gray hair and glasses, the time has come to tell my stories.

The book is divided into five sections—my youth and early teaching years in Atlanta, my five years working as a ballet accompanist and opera coach in Germany, my mature years as a piano professional in higher education and church work, my years of summer adventures as an operetta coach and professional accompanist at the American Institute of Musical Studies in Graz, Austria, and the final phase of my life—my years as a retiree, during which the adventures continue to unfold. This book is dedicated to all those unique individuals who have made my life so much fun!

My Youth and Early Teaching Years

From the Cornfield to the Opera House

When I was five years old, I lived on my grandmother's farm in Mississippi. My older sister rode the school bus to an elementary school located many miles away from the farm. She was taking piano lessons at school, but we had no piano for her to practice at home. Across the cornfield from our farmhouse was a building called the community house, where families in the community gathered for potluck suppers, quilting bees, etc. There was a big upright piano there that had belonged to my great aunt. This became my sister's first practice piano. Naturally, I tagged along, never dreaming that years later, I would be playing in the orchestra pit of the Hamburg State Opera House.

Beginnings

I began formal piano lessons when I was seven years old, although I had been playing for over a year as my sister loved to teach me pieces that she had already learned. My favorite was a masterpiece called "Little Brook," from John Thompson's red book, *Teaching Little Fingers to Play*. My elementary school had three piano teachers—all of them old as they had gray hair and glasses, just as I do now. Our piano lessons were scheduled during school hours in a large room with an upright piano. My elderly piano teacher was Miss S——. I had two lessons a week for which my mother paid fifty cents a lesson. Miss S—— had a wooden metronome on top of her piano. I hated that ticking thing. It never seemed to keep a steady beat. It was always slowing down! (Or was I speeding up?) Miss S—— brought her lunch to school, and sometimes my lessons were during her lunch hour. She had tuna between her teeth when she made corrections to my pieces. I have never liked tuna since then.

My first piano recital

Piano Recitals

Every year beginning at age eight I played in *the recital.* In January or February my piano teacher brought out a stack of new pieces and I could choose my favorite to play in *the recital*—that program at the end of the year at which the children are marched onto the stage one by one to play their *recital piece.* The children are frightened of falling apart, the teacher is afraid of being let down, and the parents are afraid of being mortified by their child's performance.

Our teacher always had a rehearsal on the stage on the day before *the recital.* The girls would wear their "hoop slips" to practice sitting down on the bench without letting the hoop slip swing out to the audience and reveal too much. But alas, sometimes a child didn't quite get it right. You could always tell the parents of that child. They were the ones with the red faces.

We always sat backstage in the order of the difficulty of our pieces—from very easy to advanced. One year, there was a little girl ahead of me who had the most beautiful green formal dress. Her grandmother was our town's professional seamstress, and she had made the beautiful dress. Sadly, I looked at my hand-me-down dress. The little green-dressed girl marched out to play, promptly had a memory slip, and sobbed in front of the audience.

I stood up to my full height and thought to myself, *I may have a hand-me-down dress, but no one will ever know that I messed up!* Sure enough, I messed up but kept going. After the recital, my mother said, "Your piece was really short this year."

"I left out three pages, Mother," I said.

Strapless Dress

In my senior year in high school, I played a solo recital. I decided to wear a lovely gold strapless dress (no bra needed). As I played my Bach piece, I noticed that my dress was more "comfortable" than usual. Uh-oh! It had come unzipped on the side away from the audience, and the only thing holding it together was a tiny hook and eye at the top. After the Bach piece, instead of getting up to bow, I stayed on the stool, nodded in the direction of the audience, then throwing my hands in the air as if in a dramatic emotional outburst, drew my right hand slowly up my left side, zipped the dress, then brought my hands crashing down on the keys to begin a dramatic Chopin Polonaise. I *never again* wore a strapless dress to play in a concert.

My First Job

After graduate school, I married my opera singing sweetheart and we moved to Florida. My husband, Tom, taught high school choral music and I traveled to an elementary school about forty miles away, where the principal was Mr. Carter (pronounced *cah-ta*), Jimmy Carter's cousin. He hired me because I could play the piano. I had been steeped in Bach, Mozart, and Chopin for the past six years in college and graduate school and knew nothing about teaching elementary music. But at least it was music, and my other choice was to be a typist at my husband's high school.

I taught music to everyone from kindergarten through sixth grade, and I had a class of "exceptional children," whom I assumed to be gifted children. *No!* These were the children with some learning challenges. I mistakenly had passed out sixth grade music books to them. "We had second grade books last year," they said.

I decided to put on a musical production with my sixth-grade class, using my entire year's budget of $25 to produce *Cowboy on the Moon*, using homemade sets and costumes. It was such a success that the exceptional children's class also wanted to present a musical. They wrote it themselves, with the main author casting himself as the lead vampire cowboy. We placed one of the boys in a "coffin" where he would rise as a vampire. There were several powder puffs in there, and the audience could see the powder rising from the coffin as he "rose out of the coffin" with his powdered white face. The only actual music in the show was the vampire riding off on his horse at the end, singing "O, Susanna!"

Puppeteer Years

We moved to Atlanta, where we lived and taught for nine years. As a young teacher, I performed a number of piano programs for children. In order to make the program more educational and visual for them, I partnered with a professional puppeteer. I explained to the children that the composers would introduce two themes in the music (two puppets), and then sometimes, they would repeat the theme but change it a little. Therefore, the puppets would come back with a different hat or wig. As I played, my partner would move the puppets—dancing across the puppet theater. The program was introduced by an elderly well-dressed puppet who introduced me as Mrs. Busyfingers, who would be playing some selections on the piano. We performed many children's shows. In one show, I played the Mozart "Variations on Twinkle, Twinkle, Little Star," and my partner made many different stars on sticks called rod puppets. For each variation, there was a different star puppet. Once, we performed for three-year-olds! I panicked. There is *no way* they would listen to these complicated Mozart variations. Surprise! As I played, the children kept singing "Twinkle, Twinkle, Little Star" for each variation. Never underestimate the ears of three-year-olds!

A Creative Student

One of my most creative students was R——, who was ten years old and full of talent. She wrote one of the songs for my puppeteer piano recitals: "I love cheese in the morning, cheese at night. Cheese in the shower, Oh, what a fright! Cheese on practically everything I eat. It's my favorite dish, and it can't be beat. Cheese. Cheese. Cheese… I love cheese."

One time, I took her to a symphony concert. After a while, she became bored and started to slowly rip her program—*rrrrrr…ip*. Glare from me. *Rrrrr…ip*. Bigger glare from me. Finally, she timed a loud cough while giving the thing a final big rip!

One lesson was most "memorable." R— had blown a large bubble gum bubble in the car. Her sticky hands and face were a fright. "She's all yours," her mother said.

She enjoyed bringing me gifts to the lessons, all beautifully wrapped in paper and ribbon—one day, an old banana peel, and one time, a burned rib. She composed creative songs about all her gifts.

Her little sister, M——, was also a joy. She never practiced, but I adored her as a person. I used to bribe her and use all my wiles to get her to practice. One day, I said, "M—, why don't we just be friends, and I'll come over to your house and play—but don't make me have to listen to you play the piano!" She started to cry and said, "But Mrs. King, I love my lessons!"

Youth Meets Middle Age

When I was about twenty-five, I taught an adult beginning student of fifty-five, who informed me that he wanted to learn to play Chopin. Mr. S— was the CEO of his company, always nicely dressed in a gray suit that matched his gray hair, stood very straight and tall, but was very stiff in his arms and wrists. He was not used to taking orders, especially from someone as young as I. One day, full of exasperation, I said, "Mr. S—, you may be the head of your company, but *I'm* the expert here!" Very meekly he said, "Yes, Ma'am."

Red Light, Green Light

One of the first jobs I had in Atlanta was as a church organist. In the nine years we lived there, I played in a variety of churches of several different denominations. One minister would say, "Let us pray," and lean over to me and say, "Play some praying music." I would choose a key and noodle around softly. My improvisational skills improved tremendously.

I also learned to think quickly. In one church, I asked the minister, "What are the hymns today?" He said, "I wait for the Spirit of God to tell me what to sing." I said, "What do you think the Spirit of God will have you sing today?" The same minister told me that he always had a long prayer, and that he wanted me to play quietly during his prayer. The Spirit of God would tell him when to stop.

"Will the Spirit of God also tell me when to start and stop?" I asked.

"No," he said. "I have lights under the pulpit. I punch the green light to tell you to play and the red light to stop."

My performance of "Silent Night"

Playing the Cello

During our first year in Atlanta, we bought season tickets to the Atlanta Symphony. Because we bought tickets in the fall, all the seats on the left (so I could see a pianist's hands) were already sold, so our tickets were on the right side, where we could see the cellos very clearly. I loved the sound and decided to take cello lessons. Tom refused to buy me a cello, so we rented one. "I'll give you six months," he said.

Playing a stringed instrument is not as easy as it looks, but I persevered. Around Christmastime, some of his music students visited our apartment. "Let me play my cello for you," I said and screeched my way through "Silent Night." They listened politely.

Several weeks later, the orchestra teacher at the high school where Tom taught invited me to play the harpsichord on the Bach, *Brandenburg Concerto No. 5*. Some of my husband's choral students saw me in the orchestra room talking with the teacher, and after I left, they cornered her: "Is Mrs. King going to play the cello with the orchestra?"

With a twinkle in her eye, she said, "Oh, yes! I heard she was taking lessons, so I thought it would be good to have another cellist in the orchestra."

They said, "Have you heard her play? She's terrible."

Coaching a Student for a Beauty Pageant

When students play in required piano recitals, they often come meekly onstage, take a timid bow, then sit at the piano, staring at the keys, then begin. Afterward, they calmly stand up, take a timid bow, then shuffle offstage. One of my advanced students told me that she was going to be in a beauty pageant, and for her talent presentation, she wanted to play the piano. This calls for a different style of piano playing.

1. Come onstage with confidence as if you were an Amazon woman about to conquer a large monster with *big* teeth (the piano).
2. Rather than standing at the *front* of the piano bench to bow, come to the *back* of the bench, and take a full, frontal "assault" bow.
3. The bench should not be parallel to the piano, as in a piano recital, but turned at a forty-five-degree angle so that the audience sees, not your face in profile, but at an angle so that you can easily turn and smile at the audience.
4. Sit down on the bench with a graceful motion. With a large sweeping gesture, spread your lovely flowing gown over the piano bench so the folds form a shimmering cover to the bench.
5. As the piece begins, do not put your hands in your lap, but rather make graceful gestures like a dancer, and with powerful arms, come commandingly down on the piano keys.
6. As you play, occasionally throw your arms in the air. Smile often at the audience, showing your beautiful, smiling face and the great joy you find in playing the piano.
7. Always end the piece with a large, fortissimo chord, and leaping to your feet in ecstasy, end in triumph as the audience screams with pleasure.
8. As you leave the stage, always keep your body at an angle so that your beautiful face is shown to the audience. Practice walking at an angle so the audience never sees your backside.

And that's the way to win a beauty pageant, playing the piano. (I coached a student to participate in the Junior Miss Pageant using these guidelines. My sister happened to be the judge. She said, "I knew exactly which student was yours because she plays exactly as you do!")

A Harpsichord for Kate

I found a small harpsichord for sale that was being sold by a dentist who had built it from a kit. We went over to his house to pick it up, and he was making final adjustments—with parts strewn all over the living room floor. It was beautifully inscribed inside "To Kate, with Love," as he had built it for Kate, his previous girlfriend, who played the harpsichord. However, he married Laura, who did not play the harpsichord and who told him to get rid of Kate's harpsichord! While the dentist and my husband, Tom, worked on getting the harpsichord back together, I talked with Laura. They had two precious children, both aged about two or two and a half, who were little screaming terrors—totally out of control. They were both adopted. As we chatted, I asked Laura, "Why two children about the same age?"

She said, "Do you know how precious a six-month-old infant looks? And the lawyer said he had a second baby for me, so I immediately said yes! Unfortunately, they both reached their terrible twos at the same time."

"What do you do while they're coloring all over your walls?" I asked.

She replied, "I drink!"

A Sad Story

One of my students was a fourteen-year-old girl named T——, who had a beautiful musical talent but had never been taught the "mysteries" of rhythm by her previous teacher. I explained to her and her mother that we were going to roll up our sleeves and tackle the problem. The lessons were long and tedious, and we were often in tears of frustration at the end. Finally, she understood the rhythmic concepts—giving her an artistic freedom she had never known. In gratitude, her mother gave me a beautiful Spanish Cascades porcelain figure of a little piper, which is on my mantle to this day. Her lessons became a source of joy rather than frustration. A few months later, T—— called me and said, "Mrs. King, I can't come to piano today. My mother died suddenly this morning of a cerebral hemorrhage." I went out in the backyard and wept. In spite of this fourteen-year-old child's grief, she had called her piano teacher.

To Quit or Not to Quit

My student, M——, was not very gifted in music but was a bright boy nevertheless. I had hopes he would grow up to be a wealthy businessman who would be a patron of the arts because of his wonderful early exposure to music. I praised his feeble efforts and gave him lots of easy pieces that never progressed in difficulty. One day, he said he wanted to play saxophone in the band, but he would have to give up piano. Seeing a way out of teaching him, I said, "Oh, you'll love band. It's so much fun! Piano is so *lonely*—always practicing by yourself!"

"I'll think about it and let you know," he said. Next week he came to the lesson and said, "I've made my decision. I've decided to stick with piano. And guess what, my sister is coming back to piano." (The sister was equally ungifted.) "And my mom is buying us a new grand piano." What's a piano teacher to do?

Playing with the Emory Wind Ensemble

I played keyboard instruments with the Emory University Wind Ensemble. The conductor would pass out new parts to the orchestra. "Do you have a piano part?" I asked.

"No, but here's a harp part." So I played the orchestral harp part on the piano.

Next piece: "Do you have a piano part?" I asked.

"No, but here's a harp part."

Next piece: "Do you have a harp part?"

"No," he said, "but here's a score. Make it up."

A Memorable Wedding

I was organist/choir director at a Methodist church in Atlanta for a year or so. One of my choir members (in her early twenties) was getting married and asked me to play for the wedding. She was marrying a man in his midforties. All was fine until she said his past girlfriend had been threatening them, so they had switched the wedding to an earlier date.

The wedding was a small simple one. The church had a single aisle, and the organ was situated in the middle of the choir loft in the front. By turning to my left as I played, I had a good view of the young bride as she came down the aisle. All of a sudden, the old girlfriend burst into the church screaming and interrupted the proceedings. The minister turned to me and said, "Play something pleasant," so I launched into Bach's "Jesu, Joy of Man's Desiring." Meanwhile, the woman ran behind the piano in one corner of the church and threatened to knock the glasses off the minister's face when he tried to make a citizen's arrest. The ushers chased her around the church, including a mad dash behind the organ where I was located. Finally, after many threats, they got her out of the church and we continued with the service, but the reception was thankfully cancelled. My comment to the bride after the service was, "At least you didn't marry someone that no one else wanted."

The former organist's comment to me was, "Oh, Vicki, you get all the *good* weddings!"

Playing at the Kennedy Center

In 1979, I decided to enter a competition for the promotion of music by Black composers. The winner would play at the Kennedy Center in Washington, D.C., on the First Annual Black Music Colloquium. I called the woman in charge and asked if you had to be Black to enter. She chuckled and said, "No." I spent several weeks delving into scores written by Black composers, discovering some beautiful music that I didn't know existed.

In the competition, the entrants had to play a full concert, with half of the music being by Black composers. One of the pieces I chose was "Sonatina for Piano" written by a New Orleans composer named Roger Dickerson. I worked for months, entered the competition, but unfortunately, did not win. A couple of months later, I got a call inviting me to come to the Kennedy Center to play Dickerson's "Sonatina," honoring Mr. Dickerson. It seems that I was the only entrant who had played the "Sonatina." They would fly me to Washington and fly Mr. Dickerson there, where we would be guests at a gala dinner honoring the composers and performers. I was thrilled!

In preparation, I played the piece for guests, for local music clubs, and for my church choir. I performed it all over Atlanta for anyone who would listen! The Kennedy Center concert was broadcast on National Public Radio. Not knowing exactly when it would be aired, I was determined to have a recording. I put a small tape recorder in my purse, covered it with a scarf, and put it in the dressing room backstage under the loudspeaker from the auditorium so that I would have a record of my performance! What a thrill to play there and meet Mr. Dickerson and many of the other famous Black composers and performers of the day.

Some months later, because of my participation in the colloquium, I received a telephone call inviting me to be listed in the book *Who's Who Among Black Musicians in America.* "Sorry," I said. "I don't qualify. I'm White!"

The Show Must Go On

My first experience in the theater was as a pussy willow in the elementary school production of *Over the Garden Wall*. In high school, I got to slap a cute boy in our drama club play. In college, I had to be a cactus in our college review that the juniors produced as a gift to the senior class.

Most of my theatrical experience came from sitting in the audience watching or playing for rehearsals, watching other people sing, dance, and act on the stage. I played for a couple of small opera companies in Atlanta as well as a lot of high school musicals. In my final Atlanta production, I was hired as the accompanist for the chorus of the rehearsals of Puccini's *La bohème*. I put the small children's chorus together and rehearsed their part in the second act. The children kept asking me what their part would be like. I said, "The stage director will probably have you do this or that." The week of the production with final rehearsals in sight, I still didn't know what the director would do. As it turned out, the director got sick. On Sunday before the Tuesday rehearsal with everybody—leads, chorus, and children—the artistic director called me and said, "We still don't have a stage director. We do have a conductor, but no one to put it all together." I suggested a new person who had just moved to Atlanta and began to look forward to Tuesday's rehearsal, in which I would play the piano, along with another pianist.

On Tuesday afternoon, I was teaching my piano students when the phone rang. The artistic director said, "Vicki, you're all we've got. You have to direct the show."

I totally panicked. I had only two hours to get to a rehearsal of an opera I had never seen, and I didn't even know Italian except *pizza* and musical terms such as *adagio*. Tom suggested that he drive me to the rehearsal to enable me to study my score with Puccini's stage directions.

"Start with the second act—the café scene—that's the one you know best."

I cast him as a waiter in the café as an extra, and he promised not to give me any suggestions about how I was doing until we got home (Tom had been in many operas and Broadway shows and had directed several musicals).

We arrived at the rehearsal. About one hundred people (or so it seemed to me) were assembled on the stage—leads, chorus, and children. The artistic director looked at the singers, who were smiling in anticipation, and said, "Vicki King will be our stage director for the show." Total silence. One hundred faces lost their smiles until I started in my well-organized way—"You do this, you do that, you come from here, you stand there."

Well, believe it or not, everybody pulled together, and we had a wonderful show. Several years later, I saw *La bohème* on the stage, and my production actually looked like it was supposed to have looked!

The Car Pool

I taught a talented red-haired boy named B——. His mother brought him to lessons, but his father's car pool picked him up. One of my neighbors said, "Vicki, every Thursday afternoon, I see four nicely dressed men sitting in a car outside your house. It's bizarre!"

When we moved to Germany, B—— and his family agreed to "babysit" my grand piano during our adventure—which lasted five years. On the day before we flew to Europe, B——'s mother called and said, "I thought you'd like to hear your piano one last time," and I heard B—— playing my piano through my tears.

Go for It!

Tom dreamed about being an opera singer in Germany. We heard about the American Institute of Musical Studies (AIMS) in Graz, Austria, and decided they could help us break into the German theater system, where every medium-sized town had an opera company, thus affording numerous opportunities for singers, pianists, dancers, orchestral musicians, and actors. We auditioned and were accepted into the AIMS program, so in June of 1980, we sold our home on Friday, had a garage sale on Saturday, and flew to Europe with one-way tickets on Sunday. We worked in Germany for five years and loved it—fulfilling the dream. Many of our adventures are included in the following stories.

WORKING IN GERMANY

The Ballet Photographer

My first job in Germany was to play for the ballet in the theater in Oberhausen. The ballet master was excited to finally have a real pianist and not just someone who "beat" the piano each day. He chose to choreograph "Pictures at an Exhibition" by Mussorgsky, a *very* difficult piece for piano, and I was thrilled with the challenge to perform it. One of the performances was in a *Gymnasium*—a high school. It was important for me to see the dancers as I played, so I turned the piano at an angle for good sight lines. A photographer from the local paper came in to take pictures of the dancers in the middle of the performance. He decided that the best place to take his photographs was close to the keyboard, which blocked my sight line!

Click! Click! Click! went the camera as I was playing this difficult piano piece. I was livid! I decided that the time had come to "change" my piano technique. No longer would I play with my fingers quietly placed on the keys. Today, I would be a flamboyant pianist who flailed my hands in the air in large emotional outbursts. One of my flailing gestures hit the photographer in his camera. He moved!

Land of Smiles

The first year in Oberhausen, I was assigned to substitute for another pianist to play celesta in the orchestra for several performances of the Franz Lehár operetta, *Land des Lächelns* (Land of Smiles). (The celesta is a keyboard instrument that is so familiar to audiences through "Dance of the Sugar Plum Fairy" from Tchaikovsky's *The Nutcracker Suite*.) I never got to play an orchestral rehearsal. I simply sat in the orchestra pit near the pianist for a couple of performances and listened.

In addition to playing the celesta, the pianist had to run upstairs and play a piano backstage. When the soprano onstage sat down at a fake piano, it was actually a real pianist in the wings who was playing. I played a couple of performances, and even though my first entrance didn't occur until later in the operetta, I always went early to practice, check that I had a music stand, etc. One night, I went to the opera house early. I went to the orchestra pit—no celesta in sight. I ran to the stage manager who said, "Frau King, it's a good thing you came early! We'll move that celesta right now!" (Special note: I found that many of my orchestra colleagues prided themselves on coming into the orchestra pit only seconds before they had an entrance. After all, they had to play the piece fifty-two times over the course of a season, so why be early?)

Which One Was it?

Our ballet company presented several performances of Prokofiev's *Romeo and Juliet*. I played the piano part in the orchestra, then ran down the hall behind the orchestra pit and up the stairs to go backstage to play the organ for the big romantic pas de deux. The only organ our theater had was an old pump organ that wheezed and groaned as I played. I'm sure it was very funny to see me pumping! One of the stagehands, unseen by the audience, thought it was great fun to "conduct" me as I played. I found it very distracting and complained to my ballet master.

At the next performance, after I finished playing the organ and was headed back to the orchestra pit, the stage manager motioned to me. I saw six stagehands, all lined up like criminal suspects in a police lineup. They all wore green coveralls and had red faces and beer bellies from drinking too much good German beer. "Frau King," the stage manager said, "which one was it?" I mumbled something about it being dark, and I wasn't sure, etc., etc. (they all looked alike!) Needless to say, the guilty man never bothered me again.

The Clean Piano

The choir director at the opera house was also the conductor of a community choir and they would be performing a concert at a restaurant in a small town in central Germany. He asked me to accompany the choir on some fairly difficult Brahms songs.

We arrived at the restaurant (called a *Gasthaus*—"guest house"). I didn't have an opportunity to play the piano, but I noticed it was a large upright. The *Putzfrau* (cleaning lady) came over to me and said, "Frau King, I cleaned the piano really nicely for you. I oiled it really well. It will look good in the spotlights." Oil? It did look really shiny. Oil? I started playing for the choir. Horror of horrors! She had oiled the keys! I spent the whole concert trying to keep my oily fingers on the keys.

After the concert, the choir had a great time enjoying the local beer. I began to be concerned about all of them driving home. About midnight, several cars driven by teenagers began to arrive. "Who are they?"

Someone said, "Oh, those are the children of the choir members, who are the designated drivers to drive their parents safely home."

Petrushka

The ballet master decided to choreograph *Three Movements from Petrushka* by Igor Stravinsky since he knew I was up for the challenge. I told my opera coach friend, D——, "I have a new piece that I will perform with the ballet in five weeks."

D—— said, "My gosh, Vicki, do you know how hard that is?" (Actually, it is what pianists refer to as a knuckle breaker!) One of the dancers' steps happened when I had a big glissando, which involves turning the hand and skimming across the keys with the back of the hand on the tips of the fingernails. Glissandos sound thrilling, but they aren't hard. It is just boring to play thirty-one times in a row! We rehearsed it over and over, and the dancers couldn't seem to perfect the step sequence.

One day, after playing the glissando for the umpteenth time, I jumped up from the piano and said, "The step goes like this!" and proceeded to execute the step perfectly! After that, the dancers had no more difficulty! (The underlying feeling in the room was that, if that pianist can do it, certainly, we can learn it!)

Mann oder Frau?

In our theater, I was one of three pianists. We all loved to play for auditions when new singers came to audition for our opera house. H—— said, "I want to play the German repertoire."

D—— said, "I want to play Italian repertoire."

They both said, "Vicki, you play the weird pieces!"

One time, I actually played a piece that was handwritten in blue ink! One of my tasks at the theater was to play/coach the obscure opera *Das Beschwerdebuch* (The Complaint Book) by Luciano Chailly (father of the famous conductor, Riccardo Chailly). The opera was written for a solo baritone who enters a Russian train station and reads complaints written by previous guests in the train station waiting room. I was dressed as Charlie Chaplin, complete with bowler hat and moustache. I came on stage smoking a large cigar and holding a big glass of beer, and I greeted the audience. There was an ashtray on the piano filled with water where I put my cigar during the performance. (One of the stagehands said, "Humph! A waste of a good cigar!")

At one performance at a senior center, I went to the ladies' room before the performance. An old lady came in and saw me dressed as Charlie Chaplin and shrieked with fright. "*Mann oder Frau?* (Man or woman?)"

"Woman dressed as a man," I said.

Toot-Toot!

After two years in Oberhausen, I was hired as a ballet pianist at the Hamburg State Opera Ballet. One of my duties was to play the piano and the celesta in the orchestra pit as needed, unseen by the audience. I played celesta on a piece called "Tristan" by Ernst Krenek. Some of the music was not particularly challenging as several of the winds only had a note or two to play occasionally. The bass clarinet solo consisted of "Toot, wait, wait, wait, toot, wait, wait, wait, wait, toot, etc." Several of the players, including myself, got tickled at this rather mindless solo. I guess the bass clarinetist also realized the humor. One night, after his solo, he lowered his instrument, looked over at the other winds and me and said, *"Das ist Kunst!* (That is art)"

A Lost Passport

One night at the Hamburg Opera House, I was scheduled to play the celesta in the orchestra. I went to the train station to say goodbye to Tom as he boarded the train to Graz. I would be joining him later, but first, I had to go on tour with the Hamburg Ballet to Venice. I hurried to the opera house and down into the dark orchestra pit to the celesta. I carelessly threw my open purse down on the floor. The day before my Venice tour, I realized I had lost my passport. I went back to the opera house and down into the pit. No passport. I remembered I had an old, expired passport that I had lost and later found (I'm very hard on passports, it seems). The expired passport could at least be used for identification. It was worth a try.

I got to the airport and the customs officer said, "Frau King, did you know your passport was expired?"

"Oh, no!" I exclaimed. "This is terrible (as if I didn't know)! I have to go to Venice with the Hamburg Ballet!"

He said, "Don't worry. Just go to the American consulate in Venice and get a new one." (FYI, there is no American consulate in Venice.)

When I got to Italy, the Italian customs officials barely gave my passport a glance. Ditto for the Austrian officials on the train to Austria. I finally got to Graz safe and sound, but ultimately traveled to the American consulate in Vienna to get a new passport. I have not lost a passport since!

Charlie's Good Time Band

I played with a German band for a couple of years called Charlie's Good Time Band, consisting of trumpet, drums, saxophone, tuba, and me on a big heavy electric Fender Rhodes keyboard. We played in various venues around northern Germany, playing popular polkas, waltzes, and other feel-good music. In Germany, there is a tradition when people are building a new home: to have a housewarming party when the house is half-finished—only bare walls and roof. They invite their friends for food and drink and hire a band. Enter Charlie's Good Time Band. As I arrived at the half-finished house, I realized there was no electricity for my keyboard. I asked the band leader, "What am I supposed to play?"

"Oh, I forgot to tell you," he said. "Here's an accordion."

Over New Year's Eve, Charlie's Good Time Band played on the world's largest ferry, sailing from Germany on the Baltic Sea to Helsinki, Finland. The ferry was a luxurious ship containing hotels, restaurants, and two stages. We alternated playing on one stage with another band playing on the second stage. On New Year's Eve, we had a huge storm with fifteen-foot waves, and needless to say, the ship began to lurch quite a bit. Most of the people on the ship became seasick, including all the men in the band. The female singer and I did not get sick, so we carried on with our program. At one point in the show, a huge wave tilted the stage so much that my piano slid away from me several feet away. I had to stop the show and say, "Please wait while I catch my piano!"

The German Avon Lady

We lived in Lüneburg, Germany, where Johann Sebastian Bach was a choir boy in 1700. We could see the spires of Bach's church from the front window of our apartment on the fourth floor. Tom sang in the theater there. One of his roles was Freddie in *My Fair Lady* by Lerner and Loewe, which is sung in German. They needed extra singers in the chorus, so I joined, always glad to make a few extra Deutsche marks singing and dancing. I got to wear a red wig, which I loved! There was a time lapse between entrances, so I spent hours in the dressing room, listening to a lot of mindless German chatter. One of the chorus ladies was an Avon representative (pronounced *Ah-fawn* in German!). She told us about visiting a farmhouse and trying to sell the *Hausfrau* some moisturizer. The farm wife (a lady with a very dry, wrinkled face) was outraged! "When I need moisturizer, I go to the barn and get some buttermilk from the cow and slap it on my face!"

Me in my red wig in *My Fair Lady*

Four Bulgarian Cockneys

In the production of *My Fair Lady*, the flower girl, Eliza Doolittle, speaks a type of broken English known as Cockney. It is very raucous with a lot of dropped consonants and harsh-sounding vowels. Professor Higgins takes Eliza in hand and teaches her to speak properly to pass her off as a high-class lady. In German theater productions of *My Fair Lady*, Eliza Doolittle speaks in a Berlin accent with screeching vowels, then slowly progresses to high German. There is a quartet of Cockney men who join her in the song "Wouldn't It Be Loverly?" The choirmaster at the theater needed to miss three weeks of rehearsals and asked me if I would work with the choir during his absence. No problem. My German had gotten pretty good after four years, so I felt comfortable. Part of my job was to work with the Cockney quartet on their Berlin accent. The four Cockneys were from Bulgaria. Here I was, with a Mississippi accent, living in Germany, teaching four Bulgarians to sing with a Berlin accent. Only in the theater!

Cabaret

In Lüneburg, I was cast in *Cabaret*. Tom was the lead—the Conferencier (played by Joel Grey in the movie). There was a small combo of girls onstage. I played an upright piano on a platform high above the stage with three other girls—a drummer, trombone player, and a saxophone player. We were all dressed as nightclub girls—I was in purple wearing a blond wig and always got to start the band playing with my very high voice yelling, "Eins, zwei, eins, zwei, drei, vier!" Tom and I developed quite a following and presented a memorable picture—he on the stage in his whiteface makeup and glitzy tuxedo and I sitting high above the stage at the piano. I always got a good laugh from the audience!

THE AMERICAN INSTITUTE OF MUSICAL STUDIES (AIMS) SUMMER PROGRAM IN GRAZ, AUSTRIA

Do You Ever Get Nervous?

During my very first summer at the AIMS program, I was backstage at one of the student recitals, along with several other pianists. A singer asked, "Do any of you pianists play the organ?"

"I do," I said.

"Good. Several of us are going to Deutschlandsberg to their church to provide special music for this Sunday's Mass, and I need someone to accompany me on the Mozart 'Alleluia' from the motet *Exsultate Jubilate*," she said.

"No problem," I said. "I've played it many times."

One of our AIMS patrons picked us up at our dorm—the singer, Tom, a harpist, and me. We arrived at the church but couldn't get in to see the organ as there was already an earlier Mass in progress. About five minutes before our Mass, we went up in the balcony at the back of the church where the organ was located. The organ was placed at the front of the balcony, and I noticed there were many pieces of red tape, marking *x*'s over certain knobs (the stops you pull to play certain sounds—flutes, trumpets, etc.). The *x*'s meant those stops didn't work. I also noticed there was no local organist there to play the Mass—hymns, responses, etc. (We had only been asked to furnish special music.)

I asked the priest in my best German, "Where is the organist?"

"He's sick (*Der ist krank*)."

"Who will play?" I asked.

"You will," he said.

I panicked. My German was terrible. The organ looked like it was on its last peep. I had only played a couple of Catholic masses in my entire life.

"I don't know the service and when to play," I said.

"No problem, the local English teacher will be here to translate for you. In the last Mass, all we had was a child who played with one finger."

Unfortunately, the English teacher didn't know the Mass well or music very well. I began to play the opening hymn in my usual quick American tempo. The cavernous church had a ten-second reverberation, so the singing in the church below lagged behind my organ playing. At one point in the service, I began to play, and the priest far below waved his arms frantically like a referee when the ball goes out of bounds. "Oops! Wrong time."

I managed to get through the service, but I was totally terrified. My husband thought it was funny and recorded the entire service. He laughed about the whole experience. (It took me ten years to get up the courage to listen to that recording!) At the end of the service, the English teacher looked at me frantically and said, "Pos-toooo-loooode."

What? Oh, postlude!

People ask me if I ever get nervous when I play. "No," I reply, "because the worst thing that could have ever happened to me already happened!"

Me playing the organ in Austria at Deutschlandsberg

Operetta Coach

I spent many summers in Graz, where some of my duties included coaching operetta arias for the singer participants. Our American singers were excited to learn the beautiful music of Austrian light operas that had been written by Johann Strauss Jr., Franz Lehár, and the native Grazer, Robert Stolz. My job was to play the piano and help the singers learn the performance practices of this music. I was able to perform in many different venues—concert halls, small auditoriums at the hospital, hotels, street corners, house concerts, and even at the local national prison. I got a newspaper article written about my prison performance! The keyboard I played belonged to an inmate, who had been an opera coach. His crime? Murdering a soprano! Hmmmm…

Pump Organ Career

When I was a little girl, I lived on my grandmother's farm. Her neighbor had a pump organ, and that was great fun to pump and play, never dreaming I would "pump" professionally! One summer in Graz, we presented the Rossini "Petite messe solennelle," which called for piano and—you guessed it—harmonium (or pump organ)! They positioned the organ at the front of the stage in the beautiful Minoritensaal (the auditorium of a monastery). This was in July, at the height of summer. The rehearsals went on for two hours, and as I pumped and played, sweat poured off me. Like a boxer, I had to keep a big towel nearby to dry off! From the farm to the monastery stage!

The Broken Ankle

One summer in Graz, I stepped off the curb in a hurry to catch a streetcar. Down I went on my left ankle. I hobbled to the tobacco/stationery store at the next corner, where I knew the owner. I asked her to call our dorm down the street. She reached our doctor, who gave me a couple of Tylenol and took me to the hospital. After the x-ray, the doctor shook his head sadly—broken ankle. He wanted me to take off my slacks to put on a cast.

"Just cut them open," I said. I couldn't go out into the world wearing only my underwear and a cast!

Meanwhile, Tom came to the hospital. "Go get some crutches from the storage room of our dorm and meet the ambulance at the door so I can walk from the ambulance to the elevator."

Back in my room that afternoon, I was visited by a friend who was a breast cancer survivor. We took pictures—me with my cast and my friend without her wig, sporting a bald head. What a pair we were!

Two days later, I played a concert for our operetta evening. I had a lovely red velvet upholstered footstool to prop up my foot. A tuxedoed escort helped me onto the stage—me in my evening gown and a cast on my foot (a chalky cast) that left marks on the stage for several years to come. I was well-known in the neighborhood after that. The Catholic diocese even put an article about me in their newsletter.

Later that week, I played the organ at a large church. Churches in Austria were built hundreds of years ago with organs located in the balcony—up narrow, winding, stone steps. This was a challenge with crutches, believe me.

I was supposed to have the cast removed before going back to the United States, but I decided to keep it on because I wanted first-class treatment on the plane. Plus, I thought my American orthopedic surgeon would enjoy seeing my Austrian walking cast.

Conducting in Vienna

Another summer, a former student of mine asked if I would conduct a Haydn Mass at St. Stephen's Cathedral in Vienna—the mother church of the Roman Catholic Archdiocese of Vienna and a beautiful example of Gothic and Romanesque styles of architecture. We had an instrumental ensemble, four singers, and my student played the organ. The various parts of the Mass were to be interpolated into the service. We arrived early, rehearsed, and then I decided to go outside the building to the ladies' room before the Mass began.

As I came back into the cathedral, I realized that the area where we were performing had been roped off to separate us from the many tourists who always visited St. Stephen's Cathedral. A serious-looking Austrian guard was there, keeping onlookers out of that area. He looked at me and said in German, "Tourist?"

I stood up straight to my five-foot, three-inch height and said gruffly (also in German), "Conductor!" and marched into the roped-off area.

At the end of the service, my student said, "Frau King, would you like to play the organ postlude?" (For the gawking tourists? Of course, I would!).

Afterward, he said, "By the way, I forgot to mention—the entire service was broadcast live on Austrian National Radio."

Playing in Austria on Christmas Eve

In 2003, the founder and artistic director of our AIMS program died. My husband, Tom, took over as artistic director and decided that we should assure the people of Graz that our AIMS program would continue for many years. As a goodwill gesture, we flew to Graz in December and organized a concert at Christmastime in which faculty and former students would participate. In addition, Tom and I wanted to present special music at several Graz churches. We decided to invite our friend N——, who is an incredible soprano (and former AIMS participant), to go with us and perform.

At the first of three masses on Christmas Eve, we provided special music in a large church in downtown Graz, where the governor of the province of Styria attended. I played the organ for a Mozart Mass at a second church, along with chorus and orchestra. Churches in Austria are not always heated, so I played the organ wearing several layers of clothing, including a heavy coat and gloves.

The third Mass of the evening was in a very old church built into the mountainside, accessible by many steps. Playing three services in a row made me quite tired, so I sat down in a comfortable chair in the balcony until it was my turn to play, falling asleep. The organist woke me up and said, "Frau King, do you want to wake up and play your organ solo?"

At the end of that service, the congregation lit candles and sang the traditional "Silent Night" but in the original German of "Stille Nacht, heilige Nacht." I looked out over that congregation from my balcony perspective and heard that lovely music with those lighted candles when all of a sudden, N—— began to sing a beautiful obligato soprano part, soaring above the congregation like an angel from heaven. I decided that life does not get much better than that!

An American Fly in Austria

As artistic director of the AIMS program, Tom flew to Graz ahead of me one summer. I flew alone to the Ronald Reagan Washington National Airport from Nashville, Tennessee. In the Reagan airport, we were transported to the main terminal in a bus. It was a sunny day, with open windows. A horsefly flew into the bus and flew into my ear. I tried to get him out, but he stayed. I went into the terminal and kept poking in my ear canal to get him out. No luck! And, of course, I didn't have any sharp objects, as they were all confiscated and there was no lag time to try to buy any cotton swabs.

I boarded the plane and asked the stewardess if they had anything to get the thing out of my ear. *No*! I tried getting some astringent out of my carry-on bag, thinking I would drown the little invader. I soaked some Kleenex with astringent and put it in my ear. Nothing. Meanwhile, the plane continued on its way to Germany. Every time the plane changed altitude the fly decided to try to crawl a bit farther in my ear. Pain! When the plane hummed along at the same altitude, the fly quieted down, and I assume, went to sleep.

Finally, we landed in Germany, and I roamed around the airport trying to find something to get it out of my ear. Nothing! The plane to Austria was a bit smaller, and again, every time we changed altitude, the fly became active. Pain! By the time I got to Graz, I was in agony. Arriving at our dorm, I told Tom, "I've got to go to the hospital and get this fly out of my ear!"

In the emergency room, they wanted to know what the problem was, and I said I had a horsefly in my ear! The poor doctor tried so hard not to laugh and said perhaps the fly wanted a free trip to Austria. She finally got it out and said she had gotten many things out of people's ears in her career, but this was the largest fly she had ever seen. Did I want it for a souvenir? Meanwhile, I had to take antibiotics for my poor infected ear, and to this day, I get very nervous when I see a horsefly—certain that he is headed for my ear!

Singing at the Graz Cathedral

AIMS developed a working relationship with the cathedral in Graz for several summers, whereby our singers provided special music for their masses. This worked well as it provided our singers a wonderful opportunity for singing in that beautiful Baroque edifice and provided music at the cathedral when their choir was on summer vacation. The cathedral always requested specific music with texts to fit the day.

One Sunday, we were to do several Heinrich Schütz duets for two sopranos, two violins, cello, and organ. I prepared the singers, and we all rehearsed on the Saturday before the Sunday mass. We all arrived on Sunday morning, ready to present the special music, *except* for one soprano. I got more and more nervous as the time came closer for the service to begin and no soprano.

At five minutes before the service, I told the organist who was to the play the service that he would need to play the organ for the special music, and I had no choice but to sing the soprano's part. At ten o'clock, the bells rang, and the priest and acolytes marched in. That was my signal for special music. I gave it my best. I'm a very faithful member of my home church choir but no soloist. Oddly, the cathedral never asked us to do special music again! (The soprano? She didn't realize Sunday streetcars ran less often, and she couldn't get there in time).

MY PROFESSIONAL
YEARS

The Student with One Arm

I taught in a community college for several years, and one of the students asked if I could teach him. He was born with a shriveled right hand, so he was only able to play with his left hand. He joined my beginning piano class and soon became a favorite of the other students. I enjoyed arranging music for him for one hand. Beginning piano pieces contain music that is quite often played with the right hand, then the left hand. One day in class, we were learning a piece for the right hand. He raised his hand and said, "Does that mean I don't have to play?"

"No, sir!" I smiled. "You simply slide to the right and your left hand is in perfect position."

Music Man

Tom and I were active in our community theater for many years. He played the leading role (Harold Hill) in the production of *Music Man*. I was the music director/ pianist for the orchestra. One of his students (T——) was the female lead of Marion the librarian. She said to him, "You know, Dr. King, that we are supposed to kiss in this show?"

"Don't worry," he said, "my wife is conducting, and there is a place in the music where the orchestra holds the note during the kiss. My wife will shorten that note!" (Another student of his, in the audience, said, "I just can't watch that kiss. It's just too weird!")

Playing the Piano with a Blue
Leg and a White Wig

One fall, our community theater produced Leonard Bernstein's *Candide*, a very impressive and difficult undertaking. I was to conduct the orchestra from the piano. The theater was rebuilt with a series of ramps and platforms, and the orchestra was placed in full view of the audience. We rehearsed for weeks as the music was quite difficult. Two weeks before opening night, I was told I needed foot surgery right away to repair a ruptured tendon in my foot or face a life with fused bones and no flexibility. What to do? I know that the show must go on!

Luckily, a very talented conductor/pianist could jump in and play the first two weekends of the shows, and I would do weeks 3, 4, and 5. So on weekend 3, I hobbled into the theater on crutches with a blue cast on my leg (my color of choice), in horrible pain, and played the show. The orchestra members were all dressed like Mozart, in period costumes and powdered wigs. So there I was, in full view of the audience, conducting and playing the piano and organ (keyboard) with my white wig and my blue leg propped up on a tall trash can! The show must go on!

Playing the Organ with a Purple Leg

I was organist-choir director at a large Methodist church during the time of my foot surgery. Little did I know I would have to be in a cast for twelve weeks and on crutches for seven months! I learned to play the organ quite well with my left foot and my injured right foot propped on a large trash can. This was fine as the organ was down in a well, behind a wooden wall, hidden from the congregation. No one saw me except my choir—until our annual community "Messiah Sing."

Several church choirs assembled at our church to sing Handel's beloved Christmas portion of the "Messiah" during the Advent season (the four weeks leading up to Christmas). During the Advent season, the church's colors were always purple, so when my doctor changed my cast, I decided to have a purple one. We had soloists, a conductor, a couple of hundred singers, and I played the organ. The wooden barrier was lifted, and the organ pulled out several feet into full view of the audience. Thus, several hundred people got the pleasure of seeing me play with a very active left foot, and a purple leg held aloft by a trash can!

More Foot Challenges

During the foot surgery period, Tom and I provided the entertainment for a dinner theater at our church. I had to do a bit of dance improvisation with my crutches, and I decided to include a couple of "foot songs" such as "Five Foot Two, Eyes of Blue" and "If You're Happy and You Know It, Stomp Your Feet."

I also acted in a play at another church, where I played the part of Madame Palestrini, an aging opera singer. One of my lines was, "How am I going to get my foot in this shoe?" and I stuck out my foot with the cast, which was, of course, *very* large and couldn't fit in *any* shoe.

We went to Albuquerque, New Mexico, that Christmas with another couple. I got first-class treatment at the airport—racing through in the "foot mobile." In Albuquerque, we rented not only a car but also a wheelchair, which was a great idea. We went up on the mesa to see the Acoma Indians do all their beautiful dances. Wheelchairs don't do well on the sand and red clay mesa with potholes everywhere. Tom was pushing my wheelchair, I was yelling, and we were racing after the other tourists to see all the Indian dances.

Look What the Cat Dragged In!

I had an older student named K——, who was a retired nurse. She practiced regularly every day and always came to lessons prepared—a teacher's dream. She followed my instructions, and I loved teaching her. One spring day during her lesson, my cat, Minnie, sneaked into the room with a little garter snake in her mouth and proudly plopped it down on the floor, next to K——'s feet.

"K——," I said softly, then raising my voice, "*get up* from the piano—*now!*"

Dutiful student that she was, she said "Okay" and got up. Then I proceeded to catch the snake and take it outside. Minnie was so proud of her "catch." A year later, the very same thing happened—same student, same cat, *different* snake!

Baseball Organist

I spent a couple of summers playing the organ for our local minor league baseball team—the Clarksville Coyotes. I even wrote the theme song for the mascot, Clark Coyote. Sitting in the announcer's booth with my keyboard, I would play a lot of "charge" riffs, plus many Mexican hat dances—the theme from *Jeopardy*, and the theme from the *Addams Family*. The pay? Free admission to the ballpark and one free hot dog. I became a vegetarian shortly after that!

A Lovely Family

M—— came to her lesson one day, and her foot was in a cast. "How did you break your foot?" I asked. *Soccer? Baseball?*

"I fell on the bottom step of your sidewalk last week as I was leaving my piano lesson." *Did she sue me?* Thank goodness, no!

M—— was not the first member of this family to take piano from me. M——'s older brother R—— took several years of piano as well. In my annual Halloween recital in the fall, my students wore costumes. R—— (fourteen years old) was playing a duet with V—— (also fourteen). Their mothers decided to dress them as Raggedy Ann and Raggedy Andy. About eight years later, these two former students called me and asked me to play for their wedding! I feel that I had a part in their romance by having them play that duet.

A Trip to China

In 1995, I was asked to go to China to tour conservatories of music as part of a piano teacher delegation through the People to People Citizen Ambassador Program. There were twenty pianists from seven countries throughout the world. It was a memorable, eye-opening experience for me—one in which I was able to share some of my ideas on natural piano technique. We visited Beijing, Guangzhou, Shanghai, and Hong Kong. We heard children play the piano, met many piano teachers (one of whom later came to the United States, and we have remained friends ever since), and toured piano factories. We usually traveled on a small bus, and I always tried to sit next to a different person on the bus to get to know my colleagues from all over the world.

We stayed in Beijing and Shanghai for ten days, with structured activities from morning to night. On the next leg of our journey to Guangzhou, our flight was about an hour and a half late because of a thunderstorm. Upon landing, we were immediately met by an oppressive humidity. By the time we boarded our bus, we were very tired and grumpy. We asked our new guide if we could just go to the hotel and rest.

"No, we are late to your next school visit," he said.

The school looked quite run-down, and there was no elevator, so we had to climb up to the third floor. We walked down a dreary hall to a classroom where, to our delight, thirty beautiful Chinese children, dressed in blue and white uniforms, and their parents had been patiently waiting for us for nearly two hours. During the ten years of the existence of this piano school, they never had visitors, and certainly not esteemed guests from the West!

We all signed their guest book and noticed they had hung balloons in the classroom to make it festive. All of the children took turns playing their pieces for us on an upright piano. They had hoped to be able to have individual lessons with members of the delegation, but there simply was not enough time. Afterward, we were so ashamed that we had complained about being too tired to experience what was, for me, one of the highlights of our trip. Seeing those children so expectant and eager to play was heartwarming. This school had very little in the way of music materials, and upon arriving back home, we sent lots of age-appropriate music to this very needy music school.

"Für Elise"—All Over the World

In over fifty years of teaching, the composition most requested by students was Beethoven's "Für Elise." Even young students seemed to be able to play the opening motive by ear. I taught piano for some years in Germany, and the German piano students requested it too. I use it as my "party piece"—a piece I can play at the drop of a hat. One section calls for a continually repeated low A. I once played on an old upright piano at a retirement home, and the piano had one sticky note. Which one? The low A, of course.

On my Chinese tour, we visited a school in Shanghai, and the children performed for us. Then the leader of the school said they would like for us to perform for them. Total silence. No one volunteered. Many of these twenty pianists were concert pianists who performed internationally. Still silence. I raised my hand and volunteered. The piano was an upright—albeit a nice new one. I sat at the piano with my long purple skirt draped around me and several children sat at my feet. I felt like Confucius. What did I play? "Für Elise," of course.

Shakespeare Adventures

Many years ago, Tom and I attended *As You Like It* at St. George's Theatre, London, and I was able to experience firsthand how music of the Renaissance was woven into the play as a prelude to the play and in scene changes, thus enhancing the drama tremendously.

Therefore, I welcomed the opportunity to research music of the period and actually be a part of a Shakespeare play. At our community theater, the Shakespearean adventures lasted over ten years. I played incidental music for several different plays, using Renaissance period instruments—recorders, a small harpsichord, and the viola da gamba (the forerunner of the cello). The viola da gamba looks like a cello except it has six strings rather than four and has frets like a guitar. I also played drums and tambourines—"A drum, a drum! Macbeth doth come!" was my cue! I loved playing low drones on my viola da gamba for ghost scenes (similar to the music of *Jaws*).

In performances of Macbeth, I played duets with a harpist. She always played unusual improvisations when Lady Macbeth began to lose her faculties—but most of the time, we played appropriate songs of the period. One Saturday night, she had to play for a wedding and told me she would be arriving late. As the play progressed, I became even more creative and played alone with all my instruments. Because the harpist didn't arrive in time for Lady Macbeth's monologue, I moved over to her harp and played strange improvisations as if I could really play. Add a harp adventure to my experiences!

Teaching Medieval Ideas

One semester, I taught a class in the honors program at a university. I wanted my students to not only read about the Middle Ages but to experience it. So when we read poetry of the period, I selected a student to put on a period costume and be the class troubadour, improvising on a small harp borrowed from one of my harp-playing friends. They, of course, had never played the harp but were quick to learn a bit as their grade depended on it.

The culmination of the class (the final exam) consisted of going to a local park with an outdoor pavilion that resembled a medieval lodge with open sides and huge cross beams for the roof. Each person was to research a character from the Middle Ages and come dressed as that character. We prepared food from the period and practiced the manners of the period, which meant eating with our fingers and using our sleeves to wipe our mouths! We danced to authentic live music from the Middle Ages provided by the local early music group that I founded and directed. Each student chose a specific, well-documented character, dressed appropriately, and addressed the assembled body in the first person: "I am _____, and I did_____," speaking as their medieval character for five minutes. Our own medieval reenactment was a great success. Ideas and concepts are best remembered if they are really experienced.

Little Shop of Horrors

I was working at a university as a staff accompanist. One of the students played the piano for a community production of *Little Shop of Horrors*. She needed a substitute for one Friday night show. So I volunteered. There would not be a rehearsal—just jump in and play the performance. She gave me the music and talked me through all my cues. At the show (which I had only seen a couple of times—once in German) the drummer sat behind me, whispering tempos to me. I also had an earphone and someone in the light booth was saying, "Play now." It was a *show* of horrors for me, but I lived through it.

The New Student

One day, I was expecting a new private piano student and her mother at my home. I told Tom to please answer the door as I was not quite dressed when the doorbell rang. He is used to my teaching adult students as well as children, so he thought nothing of it when two nicely dressed African American ladies were at our door.

"Please come in," he said, "and make yourself comfortable at the piano. Vicki will be out in a minute."

I walked into the living room, surprised to see these two ladies. They were not my expected student and her mother at all. They were Jehovah's Witnesses!

The T-shirt

The joy of piano teaching is that each student has a unique personality, which often prompts a story! I once taught two students—brother about eleven, sister about nine. Their mom always had to nag them to practice (how many times have I heard that?), so she decided to take piano herself, and guess what—the kids had to nag *her* to practice!

I always had three recitals a year to give my students much performance experience—Halloween recital, Christmas recital, and an end-of-the year recital. I allowed students to wear comfortable clothing at the spring recital, so, N—— (the eleven-year-old boy) came in wearing a T-shirt. He sat with his parents during the whole program looking like the cat who had swallowed the canary. I sat across the room from the piano in my "teacher" chair. Only when he got up to play was I able to read the back of his shirt for the first time: *Surf naked!*

A Student with Priorities

I once had a student named E——, who was a piano teacher's dream. He came regularly to lessons, practiced every day, did his assigned work, and made progress each week. He always had goals, and one of these was to earn a gold cup through the National Federation of Music Clubs program by entering festivals each year and earning points. At the end of three years of diligent work, a student could earn a gold cup engraved with his name and the year. E—— worked hard to achieve this goal and was to receive his gold cup in a ceremony at the university. To accommodate E——'s schedule that day, I asked the presenter to allow him to receive his cup first. After proudly receiving his cup, he hurried out of the auditorium to go to the airport. His father, who was in the military, was arriving home from Iraq after being deployed for over a year.

A Very Talented Student

One year, I had a very talented student named P———, who was homeschooled by his parents. He studied harp with his mother, piano with a college professor, organ with a well-known professional teacher, and was learning German in addition to regular studies. His mother asked if I would teach him harpsichord but not just harpsichord repertoire. He wanted to study figured bass, which is the Baroque art of playing from a bass line and realizing (or simply reading) the tiny numbers that constitute the harmonies. It is a specialized type of playing that was used during the time of Bach, and somewhat lost in our own time unless it is particularly cultivated and practiced by scholars. I said I was delighted and certainly up for the challenge. The punch line: the lessons were to take place in German! This is concentrated, tedious work at best but even more tedious in German! After each lesson, I would crawl away from the lessons—totally exhausted. His father said, "Now you know how we feel!"

Playing in Mexico

I was working as a choir director in a Methodist church in Kentucky and was asked to take several of my choir members on a mission trip to Mexico. We were to provide music for several worship services, for which we prepared praise choruses and upbeat spirituals. Because of my quilting hobby, I was asked to take materials to teach the Mexican women patchwork crafts that they could sell at the mission's small store.

The mission was located in a "fortress" structure that could be seen from miles away. As we traveled through the countryside, I noticed the extreme poverty of the people—many homes had only shacks made from wood and tin. Skinny dogs and pigs ran unrestrained through dusty yards.

An American missionary couple had seen the potential in this abandoned fortress and had dedicated their lives to making that space into a place where the local people could worship in the small chapel, bring their goods to sell at the market on the fortress grounds, and have space for ceramic and stained glass studios.

I was able to work on crafts with several women of the mission, and together, we made a colorful wall hanging. On a yellow background, we sewed many colorful butterflies and yo-yos (fabric sewn into a circle) in the shape of a cross.

Our group led several worship services. The mission had a small piano that I played for the services. I cherish a picture of myself playing the piano with the light streaming through the stained glass window over my head. The people of the mission had never heard this piano sound so lovely. "Could I please stay and teach them to play?"

We also took part in several church services in the area, where I played keyboards, understanding little of what was said. Our common language was music! I looked around and saw happy people. They had so few material possessions—no microwaves, no cellphones—but they possessed an inner happiness—a contentment—a joy—a strength. It made me reflect on our lives. Do we have unneeded possessions? Do we allow enough time to nourish our own souls?

The stained glass cluster of blue butterflies I bought there, now hanging in my window at home, is a constant reminder of the resurrection—from the cold of winter to the revival that spring brings—fondly remembering the abandoned fortress on a high hill in Mexico and a small village full of life and hope for the inhabitants.

The quilt wall hanging made in Mexico

A Student with an Incredible Ear

I taught at an historically Black university for many years. The majority of my students had a background in piano that consisted of playing mostly by ear in their home churches or playing the latest pop tunes. Naturally, I attempted to elevate their weak piano reading skills to match their strong piano playing aural skills. About four weeks into the fall semester, we had a large convocation, at which the faculty were all decked out in academic robes, speeches were made by dignitaries, etc. The university choir sang, and the singers were all well-known to me as I taught piano to most of them. They had a wonderful guest speaker, who closed her speech with a gospel song that I didn't know. To my surprise, I glanced up in the balcony and saw J——, one of my piano students, accompanying the guest with an extremely difficult and virtuosic accompaniment, playing with style, flair, and command. Afterward, he came by my office, and I complimented his fine playing.

"When did you rehearse with her?" I asked.

"I didn't," he said. "Dr. N—— was supposed to play for her, but he had to leave after the choir sang, so I volunteered."

"Did you know the song?" I asked.

He said, "No, but I listened to it on YouTube on my headphones during the speech."

What an amazing ear and an amazing talent!

A Five-Dollar Reward

One of the banes of a piano teacher's existence is the student who does not practice. Happy is the teacher who has a student who practices regularly and enjoys doing so. I loved teaching at the historically Black university as my students were so outgoing and lovable. But did they always practice? *No!* Some of my students were piano majors, but most of them were trombone majors, flute majors, voice majors, or saxophone majors, who had to divide their practice time between their major instrument and required piano. Piano for nonpiano majors was taught in groups—class piano.

My piano assignments were not always completed to my satisfaction! One night, I decided to patrol the practice rooms and see if any of my students were there. Jackpot! One student was practicing. So the next day in class, I announced that, out of curiosity, I had patrolled the practice rooms to monitor all the practicing and found only one student, so as a reward, I gave him $5! The others said, "What about my $5?"

"You weren't practicing," I said.

Ten Students in Europe

I lived in Germany for five years and traveled in Europe at least thirty times. When we worked at the AIMS program in Graz, Austria, we were always interacting with students. But we never had total responsibility of them in a tour situation.

In 2011, I received a grant from my university to take ten music students to Vienna and Florence. After careful planning, it all came to pass. Tom traveled ahead of us to check out our hotel accommodations, meet us at the Vienna airport, etc. I met with the ten students at the Nashville airport. I had offered $100 to the student who would bring the least amount of luggage, as I knew the joys of traveling light. One girl, J——, brought only a backpack, so she got the $100. (That didn't mean she returned home with only a backpack!) One student had huge suitcases full of ten days' worth of changes of clothing—he was *extremely* stylish.

All of my plans, of course, didn't work out perfectly. In one of our plane connections, I was sent with five students to Paris, and five students were sent to Amsterdam. Therefore, five students would travel without me to Vienna and arrive ahead of me! I called Tom on our European cell phones and told him to meet the students. (The students had never met my husband.)

"What does he look like?" they asked.

"He's a cute old guy wearing a hat with our university logo," I said.

They somehow connected, and he got them settled then came back to the airport to meet the rest of us. Apparently, I had reserved apartments in a very Orthodox Jewish sector of Vienna, and it was Friday night. Luckily, Tom secured the keys to our apartments before sundown.

One of the interesting adventures was taking ten African American students to a tiny grocery store on Saturday morning to help them shop for the weekend as the stores would be closed on Saturday afternoon and all day on Sunday. We had to follow them around in the store and translate everything they were interested in buying. We had many curious stares from the local Austrians.

We had some wonderful adventures—taking them to see *Merry Widow* at the Vienna Folk Opera House and taking them to the Musikverein to an all-Mozart concert. I can still see the lights in their eyes. We visited Beethoven's grave, and they took many pictures. We visited Schubert's birthplace, the little church where he was baptized, and the Mozart house. Each morning, they met in our apartment for a little lecture on what we would see that day.

I didn't allow them to have free time until I was sure they knew their way around the city. One time, at three o'clock in the morning, I heard loud voices out the window. Hoping it was some other group, I tried to go back to sleep. Then I recognized the voice of one of my students. My husband said, "You go. They're your students."

The overnight train trip to Florence was a challenging adventure as we were sleeping on the train and had so much luggage to store. Remember my $100 reward to the "backpack" girl? We stumbled over luggage all night!

Upon arrival in Florence, we had a delightful bus tour of the city (after storing our luggage). Then we checked into the hotel and found that half of us would be in a second hotel down the street, so the student with the heavy suitcase had to drag it several blocks over cobblestones with a broken wheel!

In Florence, we attended Mass at the cathedral, and the students were able to participate and sing the hymns. We heard a choral concert of Gregorian chant in a beautiful, domed hall from the twelfth century, heard an opera, and saw Michelangelo's *David* at the art museum.

In our final trip to the airport, I ordered two taxis, and I thought the taxi drivers were going to mutiny when they saw all our luggage. Upon arrival at the airport, the student with the big suitcase was over the weight limit, so he began parceling out jeans and shirts to other people, finally throwing some things away. (It took him weeks to retrieve all his belongings after we returned to Nashville!)

The flight home was fine until Tom, J——, and I missed one connection in Minneapolis. Nine of my students arrived in Nashville and greeted their parents—without me!

MY MATURE YEARS

Playing for Ballet as a Retiree

When I retired from university teaching, I told all my piano teacher friends that I would not be teaching anymore. They looked at me as if I had three heads. Piano teachers don't retire! They "die on the piano bench," correcting one last scale fingering! My "desire" to no longer teach lasted only a few months, then I couldn't stay away. I taught piano pedagogy to piano majors at the university in the town where we retired and observed them teaching their young students. Also, my ballet accompanist skills were needed, so I joined the accompanying staff of the university ballet department, along with several pianists young enough to be my grandchildren! I told the head of the department I would continue working as long as it was fun—and it most certainly was! I had a reason to dress up each day, walk a couple of blocks to the bus stop with my backpack full of music, ride the bus to the university along with many students, and listen to their chatter about various subjects.

At the university, I walked across campus to play for my ballet classes—sometimes making the bus/walking trip morning and afternoon. I played about eight classes per week for ballet majors, ballet electives, and the precollege ballet program. I loved planning music to fit specific steps for the classes. As the dancers executed plies, pirouettes, tendus, and grand battements, I played music from the classics, Broadway, operetta, opera, ballet, as well as music by pedagogical composers. I loved watching the dancers—how music and dance merge to create a unique art form. I heard the ballet teachers say on many occasions, "Listen to the music. Let it tell you what to do."

One of my joys was working with the late prima ballerina, Violette Verdy (1933–2016), who premiered many ballets with the great choreographer George Balanchine in the 1960s and 1970s. I selected many French pieces to play in her classes, and she often ran to the piano and remarked, in her lilting French accent, "What is that lovely music?"

The dancers and I hung on every word as she told wonderful stories about Mr. B——, as the dancers of the New York City Ballet called him, including how he would sit at the piano and play the most complicated music for his dancers and see if they could dance to it. At eighty-two, Violette was a role model for me (at seventy-one), with her energy and love of the young students. Witnessing the dancers mature and grow in their appreciation of the history of ballet, paired with great music, and watching them meet the high standards set by Violette was a pleasure for me—every day!

A Weaving for a Dancer

Each year, I am contracted to be a judge for the National Guild of Piano Teachers. I have adjudicated hundreds of piano students as they play a program of between three to twenty pieces for me—sometimes from memory, sometimes with the music, playing scales and cadences for each respective piece. Many years ago, I adjudicated in Evansville, Indiana. One of the teachers took me to dinner, along with one of her adult students, a thirty-two-year-old beginner who had been a dancer. The next day, the dancer played her program for me. She told me that she was very nervous as it was her first time to play for a judge. One of my hobbies is weaving, so I gave the dancer one of my small woven pieces.

"That's beautiful!" she exclaimed.

"Do you really think it's beautiful?"

"Oh yes," she said.

"Look closely. You'll see that it has a mistake in it. Do you still think it's beautiful?"

"Oh yes," she said.

I told her to keep the weaving on her piano as a reminder that we may make mistakes in our playing, but the overall beauty of the music shines through.

Learning from My Students

I have taught students of all levels throughout my lifetime—young and old students, beginners and advanced students, students with amazing talents, and students with only a wish to improve. Each one was unique, which reminds me of the advice of my piano pedagogy teacher in college, "We teach the child, not the subject." I have taught individuals my whole life through the medium of music—specifically, the piano. My favorite students to teach are the university students. I have learned so much from these students, especially about technology.

When I was in college, I never dreamed of calling my professors at home, yet my students today are known to text me at all hours of the day or night! I learned about PowerPoint presentations from my university students as they gave oral reports on particular composers. What creative and beautiful presentations they made! Asking one of my university piano students the meaning of a particular musical term, I watched him reach for his phone. I pulled a music dictionary from the shelf and said, "This is called a book. We'll look it up here."

He said, "For real?"

From my university students, I have learned about downloading applications—Skype, FaceTime, Zoom, and a whole host of other technological terms that were not in my vocabulary ten years ago. Like my university student from many years ago, I now find myself *googling* something on my phone several times a day! A couple of years ago, I was standing at a bus stop near the university on my way home. A student asked me what time the bus was coming. I found the app on my phone that could be downloaded for our local transit system and showed it to her. She was amazed and said, "I think it's great that someone your age can use a smartphone!"

Keeping Active During the 2020 Pandemic

During the year of the pandemic, I became quite creative as our social life, as we had known it, ceased to exist. There were no more concerts, operas, dinners with friends, or live church services. Tom and I chose to make music videos and post them on Facebook and YouTube to give us a creative outlet and to share our art. I began to teach on Zoom and FaceTime. Through one of Tom's local theater connections, we volunteered to act in a skit—one of fifteen short skits, competing for prizes. We were to be the actors, and we were assigned a playwright. We were allowed only about twenty-four hours to write the play, rehearse the play, and film the play. Our play was called *Grandits*, about two old people who meet in prison, fall in love, escape by digging their way out with a spoon, and start a new life of crime together. We had great fun, and I was awarded one of the best actress awards!

Judging Seventy-Seven Chinese Children

In my work as a judge for the National Guild of Piano Teachers, I have traveled all over the United States, evaluating children and reinforcing solid teaching techniques of teachers, plus giving teachers ideas to improve. I have judged from the West (Alaska and Arizona) to the East (New Jersey, Maryland, and Connecticut); Michigan in the North; Florida in the South; and Indiana, Kentucky, Tennessee, and Ohio in the heartland. With the advent of COVID-19 during 2020, most of the teachers chose to have their students evaluated through online platforms such as Skype, FaceTime, or Zoom.

The most unusual judging I have done in perhaps thirty years of judging was in December 2020. I judged seventy-seven children from Wuhan, China. The teachers sent video links of all the students as well as a list of the pieces they would be playing so that I could find the scores in my library. The titles of pieces were in Chinese, and I translated them with the aid of my computer, but sometimes, the translations were odd, even quite funny! For example: "Three Blind Mice" became "Three Blind Rats," "Für Elise" became "For Alice," Bach's "Musette" became "Bagpipe Dance," "Old MacDonald Had a Farm," became "Ole Wheat Has a Big Farm," and Burgmüller's "Arabesque" became "Arab Dance."

The children were all dressed up—the little girls with dresses of taffeta or silk and the little boys with bow ties. They all had a big number stuck on their right sleeve to help me identify them. One little girl was playing "Für Elise," and just as she got to the last section, her number started to slide down her arm. She looked at it sliding, stopped playing, put her number back on her arm, and continued playing. One boy missed a note, made a terrible bad face to the camera, then kept going. One boy had a big treble clef sign shaved into his hair on the piano side of his head. He obviously loved music! What a joy to hear these children in my own home—just as I had heard so many in China when I visited there so many years ago!

Coda

I never would have thought that those beginning fifty-cent lessons so long ago would have allowed me to experience such delightful adventures. I've played all over the world, met so many interesting people, and had so much fun along the way. Playing the piano opens doors that only music can. It needs no words, and it builds strong bonds, not barriers, among people. Music needs to be shared. One year, I played a Mozart quintet in Germany—I, the pianist from America, the horn player from Japan, the oboe player from Romania, the clarinet player from Australia, and the bassoon player from Germany. Music was our catalyst, we "spoke" Mozart as our language, and we bonded beautifully.

Each day for me has been interesting—full of joy, full of love, and full of music. Many of my friends have said retirement became boring, even more so during the pandemic. Not for me! There is much more music that I still want to play and so much more for me to learn.

I hope that my stories have given you a bit of a chuckle or a thought to ponder. They say that when an old person dies, a library is lost. Each person is a library. Each person has stories. Please tell your stories to your children, your grandchildren, or anyone who seems interested or needs a "lift." Better yet—write them down so that many can share your insights. Sit down and begin!

About the Author

Vicki King is a professional pianist who has taught piano students of all levels for over fifty years. She specializes in helping students overcome performance injuries. Her website is www.naturalpianoplaying.com

CPSIA information can be obtained
at www.ICGtesting.com
Printed in the USA
LVHW071333281221
707353LV00017B/665